This journal belongs to:

_____

Today is
my day.

TODAY IS MY DAY: _____

(DATE)

S M T W T F S
☑ ☑ ☑ ☑ ☑ ☑ ☑

_____

_____

_____

_____

_____

_____

_____

_____

_____

_____

_____

_____

_____

_____

_____

_____

_____

_____

_____

_____

_____

_____

_____

_____

_____

_____

_____

_____

_____

_____

_____

_____

_____

_____

_____

_____

_____

_____

_____

_____

_____

_____

_____

_____

_____

Do
you dare
stay out?

Do
you dare
go in?

TODAY IS MY DAY: _____ S M T W T F S

(DATE)

TODAY IS MY DAY: _____
(DATE)

S M T W T F S
☑ ☑ ☑ ☑ ☑ ☑ ☑

Oh!
The places
I've been!

TODAY IS MY DAY: _____

(DATE)

S M T W T F S
☐ ☐ ☐ ☐ ☐ ☐ ☐

TODAY IS MY DAY: _____

(DATE)

S M T W T F S

☐ ☐ ☐ ☐ ☐ ☐ ☐

_____

_____

_____

_____

_____

_____

_____

_____

_____

_____

_____

_____

_____

_____

_____

_____

_____

_____

I'm off to great places!

I've
discovered
new places.

TODAY IS MY DAY: _____ □ □ □ □ □ □ □

S M T W T F S

(DATE)

I've heard
the bands
playing.

TODAY IS MY DAY: _____

(DATE)

S M T W T F S
☑ ☑ ☑ ☑ ☑ ☑ ☑

I've seen great sights!

I've **soared to high** heights.

TODAY IS MY DAY: _____

(DATE)

S M T W T F S
☐ ☐ ☐ ☐ ☐ ☐ ☐

TODAY IS MY DAY: _____ ☐ ☐ ☐ ☐ ☐ ☐ ☐
(DATE)

S M T W T F S

TODAY IS MY DAY: _____

(DATE)

S M T W T F S
☑ ☑ ☑ ☑ ☑ ☑ ☑

TODAY IS MY DAY: _____
(DATE)

S M T W T F S
☐ ☐ ☐ ☐ ☐ ☐ ☐

I'm a
Success!

TODAY IS MY DAY: _____
(DATE)

S M T W T F S
☐ ☐ ☐ ☐ ☐ ☐ ☐

Ready for anything!

TODAY IS MY DAY: _____ S M T W T F S

(DATE)

TODAY IS MY DAY: _____   S M T W T F S
                              (DATE)

TODAY IS MY DAY: _____ ☑S ☑M ☑T ☑W ☑T ☑F ☑S
(DATE)

Oh!
The places
I've been!

TODAY IS MY DAY: _____

(DATE)

TODAY IS MY DAY: _____ □□□□□□□
                        (DATE)   S M T W T F S

TODAY IS MY DAY: _____

(DATE)

S M T W T F S
☑ ☑ ☑ ☑ ☑ ☑ ☑

TODAY IS MY DAY: _____

(DATE)

S M T W T F S
☑ ☑ ☑ ☑ ☑ ☑ ☑

Today is
my day.

TODAY IS MY DAY: _____

(DATE)

S M T W T F S
☑ ☑ ☑ ☑ ☑ ☑ ☑

TODAY IS MY DAY: _____
(DATE)

S M T W T F S
☑ ☑ ☑ ☑ ☑ ☑ ☑

Do
you dare
stay out?

Do
you dare
go in?

Ready for
anything!

TODAY IS MY DAY: _____

(DATE)

S M T W T F S
☐ ☐ ☐ ☐ ☐ ☐ ☐

TODAY IS MY DAY: _____
(DATE)

S M T W T F S
☐ ☐ ☐ ☐ ☐ ☐ ☐

I'm off to great places!

TODAY IS MY DAY: _____

(DATE)

S M T W T F S
☑ ☑ ☑ ☑ ☑ ☑ ☑

TODAY IS MY DAY: _____

(DATE)

S M T W T F S
☑ ☑ ☑ ☑ ☑ ☑ ☑

I've discovered new places.

TODAY IS MY DAY: _____

(DATE)

S M T W T F S
☐ ☐ ☐ ☐ ☐ ☐ ☐

TODAY IS MY DAY: _____

(DATE)

S M T W T F S
☑☑☑☑☑☑☑

I've heard
the bands
playing.

TODAY IS MY DAY: _____
(DATE)

S M T W T F S
☑ ☑ ☑ ☑ ☑ ☑ ☑

_____

_____

_____

_____

_____

_____

_____

_____

_____

_____

_____

_____

_____

_____

_____

_____

_____

_____

_____

_____

_____

_____

_____

_____

TODAY IS MY DAY: _____ S M T W T F S
(DATE)

I've seen great sights!

TODAY IS MY DAY: _____
(DATE)

S M T W T F S
☐ ☐ ☐ ☐ ☐ ☐ ☐

I've
soared
to high
heights.

TODAY IS MY DAY: _____ S M T W T F S
(DATE)

_____
_____
_____
_____
_____
_____
_____
_____
_____
_____
_____
_____
_____
_____
_____
_____
_____
_____
_____
_____
_____
_____
_____
_____
_____
_____
_____

TODAY IS MY DAY: _____

(DATE)

S M T W T F S
☐ ☐ ☐ ☐ ☐ ☐ ☐

_____

_____

_____

_____

_____

_____

_____

_____

_____

_____

_____

_____

_____

_____

_____

_____

_____

_____

_____

_____

_____

_____

_____

TODAY IS MY DAY: _____

(DATE)

S M T W T F S
☑ ☑ ☑ ☑ ☑ ☑ ☑

_____

_____

_____

_____

_____

_____

_____

_____

_____

_____

_____

_____

_____

_____

_____

_____

_____

_____

_____

_____

_____

_____

_____

_____

TODAY IS MY DAY: _____   S M T W T F S
                                                 ☑☑☑☑☑☑☑
                              (DATE)

I'm a
Success!

TODAY IS MY DAY: _____
(DATE)

S M T W T F S
☑ ☑ ☑ ☑ ☑ ☑ ☑

I've taken
the lead!

Oh!
The places
I've been!

TODAY IS MY DAY: _____
(DATE)

S M T W T F S
☐ ☐ ☐ ☒ ☐ ☐ ☐

_____

_____

_____

_____

_____

_____

_____

_____

_____

_____

_____

_____

_____

_____

_____

_____

_____

_____

TODAY IS MY DAY: _____

(DATE)

S M T W T F S

_____
_____
_____
_____
_____
_____
_____
_____
_____
_____
_____
_____
_____
_____
_____
_____
_____
_____
_____
_____
_____
_____
_____
_____
_____
_____
_____

TODAY IS MY DAY: _____ S M T W T F S

(DATE)

_____

_____

_____

_____

_____

_____

_____

_____

_____

_____

_____

_____

_____

_____

_____

_____

_____

_____

_____

_____

_____

_____

_____

_____

Do
you dare
stay out?

Do
you dare
go in?

TODAY IS MY DAY: _____
(DATE)

S M T W T F S
☐ ☐ ☐ ☐ ☐ ☐ ☐

TODAY IS MY DAY: _____ S M T W T F S
(DATE)

Ready for anything!

_____
_____
_____
_____
_____
_____
_____
_____
_____
_____
_____
_____
_____
_____
_____
_____
_____
_____
_____
_____

I'm off to great places!

TODAY IS MY DAY: _____

(DATE)

S M T W T F S

TODAY IS MY DAY: _____
(DATE)

S M T W T F S
☑ ☑ ☑ ☑ ☑ ☑ ☑

I've discovered new places.

TODAY IS MY DAY: _____

(DATE)

S M T W T F S
☐ ☐ ☐ ☐ ☐ ☐ ☐

TODAY IS MY DAY: _____   S M T W T F S
                            (DATE)   ☐☐☐☐☐☐☐

I've heard
the bands
playing.

TODAY IS MY DAY: _____

(DATE)

S M T W T F S
☑ ☑ ☑ ☑ ☑ ☑ ☑

I've seen great sights!

I've **soared to high** heights.

TODAY IS MY DAY: _____

(DATE)

S M T W T F S
☐ ☐ ☐ ☐ ☐ ☐ ☐

TODAY IS MY DAY: _____ S M T W T F S

(DATE)

_____

_____

_____

_____

_____

_____

_____

_____

_____

_____

_____

_____

_____

_____

_____

_____

_____

_____

_____

_____

_____

_____

_____

TODAY IS MY DAY: _____

(DATE)

S M T W T F S
☑ ☑ ☑ ☑ ☑ ☑ ☑

I'm a
Success!

TODAY IS MY DAY: _____ S M T W T F S
(DATE)

I've taken
the lead!

TODAY IS MY DAY: _____

(DATE)

S M T W T F S
☐ ☐ ☐ ☐ ☐ ☐ ☐

TODAY IS MY DAY: _____

(DATE)

S M T W T F S
☑ ☑ ☑ ☑ ☑ ☑ ☑

TODAY IS MY DAY: _____

(DATE)

S M T W T F S
☑ ☑ ☑ ☑ ☑ ☑ ☑

Oh!
The places
I've been!

TODAY IS MY DAY: _____
(DATE)

S M T W T F S
☐ ☐ ☐ ☑ ☐ ☐ ☐

_____
_____
_____
_____
_____
_____
_____
_____
_____
_____
_____
_____
_____
_____
_____
_____
_____
_____
_____

Published in the United States by Random House Children's Books,
a division of Random House LLC, a Penguin Random House Company, New York.

This is an adapted edition of *Oh, the Places You'll Go!*,
TM and copyright © by Dr. Seuss Enterprises, L.P. 1990,
originally published in hardcover
by Random House Children's Books in 1990.

Random House and the colophon
are registered trademarks of Random House LLC.

Visit us on the Web!
Seussville.com
randomhousekids.com
RHTeachersLibrarians.com

ISBN: 978-0-553-52189-4
MANUFACTURED IN CHINA   10 9 8 7 6 5 4 3 2 1

Random House Children's Books
supports the First Amendment
and celebrates the right to read.